LET'S TALK ABOUT

BREAKING PROMISES

REVISED FOR EDUCATIONAL USE

By Joy Wilt Berry

Illustrated by John Costanza

CHILDRENS PRESS ™

CHICAGO

Let's talk about BREAKING PROMISES.

Have your friends ever
told you they would do something
and then not done it?

5

Have adults ever
   told you they would do something
   and then not done it?

7

People who
  say they will do something
  and then do not do it
are BREAKING A PROMISE.

When someone breaks a promise to you,
    how do you feel?
    what do you think?
    what do you do?

When someone breaks a promise to you,

you may feel
disappointed and upset;

you may think that person
cannot be trusted;

you may not believe that person
the next time a promise is made.

It is important to treat others
the way you want to be treated.

If you want others
to keep their promises,
you must keep your promises.

If you keep your promises,
people will trust you.

When people trust you,

    they can depend on you;

    they know you will
not let them down;

    they know you will
be honest;

    they know you will
not lie.

It is important for people to trust you.

If people trust you,
    they will believe what you say;

    they will allow you
    to do more on your own.

If you want
people to trust you,
you must show them
you can be trusted.

To show that you can be trusted,

*be where you say you will be
when you say you will be there.*

To show that you can be trusted,

do what you say you will do.

To show that you can be trusted,

give what you say you will give.

If you want to be trusted,

you must keep your promises.

29

To be happy, treat others
the way you want to be treated.

Everyone is happier
when no one breaks promises.

About the Author

Joy Berry is the author of more than 150 self-help books for children. She has advanced degrees and credentials in both education and human development and specializes in working with children from birth to twelve years of age. Joy is the founder of the Institute of Living Skills. She is the mother of a son, Christopher, and a daughter, Lisa.